DISCARD

DEMCO

Mysterious Encounters

Poltergeists

by Katy S. Duffield

KIDHAVEN PRESS

An imprint of Thomson Gale, a part of The Thomson Corporation

Detroit • New York • San Francisco • New Haven, Conn. • Waterville, Maine • London

© 2007 Thomson Gale, a part of The Thomson Corporation.

Thomson and Star Logo are trademarks and Gale and KidHaven Press are registered trademarks used herein under license.

For more information, contact
KidHaven Press
27500 Drake Rd.
Farmington Hills, MI 48331-3535
Or you can visit our Internet site at http://www.gale.com

Picture Credits:
Cover: © CORBIS; © Bettmann/CORBIS, 10, 26; © Hulton-Deutsch Collection/CORBIS, 12; © Guy Lyon Playfair/Fortean Picture Library, 16; Nina Leen/Time-life Pictures/Getty Images, 29, 31; The Kobal Collection, 5; © Mary Evans Picture Library, 35; © Mary Evans Picture Library/The Image Works, 6, 9, 15, 18, 21, 25, 27, 34, 37

LIBRARY OF CONGRESS CATALOGING-IN-PUBLICATION DATA

Duffield, Katy.
  Poltergeists / by Katy S. Duffield.
    p. cm. — (Mysterious encounters)
  Includes bibliographical references and index.
  ISBN-13: 978-0-7377-3665-6 (hardcover)
  1. Poltergeists—Juvenile literature. I. Title.
  BF1483.D84 2007
  133.1'42—dc22
                                                                2007006888

ISBN-10: 0-7377-3665-8

Printed in the United States of America

Contents

Chapter 1

Noisy Spirits

A lamp floats through the air. Four chairs mysteriously appear, balanced atop a small kitchen table. Bite marks become visible on a person's body. Each of these events occurred in Steven Spielberg's classic film *Poltergeist*. Although the *Poltergeist* film is fictional, numerous accounts of suspected **poltergeist** activity have been reported throughout history in many parts of the world.

What Is a Poltergeist?

The word *poltergeist* comes from two German words. The word *polter* means "noise" or "racket." The word geist means "spirit." Since poltergeists are usually heard and not seen, the name "noisy spirit" is a good fit for these menacing beings. Noises caused by poltergeists may begin as the sound of footsteps, scratches, taps, or raps. The noises may then progress to loud bangs or crashing sounds.

One example of a poltergeist's noisemaking ability took place in Tedworth, England, in 1661. As author Elliott O'Donnell writes, "[The Tedworth poltergeist] . . . awoke everyone at night by thumping on doors and imitating beatings of a drum. It rattled bedsteads, scratched on the floor and wall as if possessing iron talons, groaned, and uttered loud cries of 'A witch! A witch!'" [1]

A scene from the 1982 film *Poltergeist,* the fictional tale of a family haunted by poltergeists.

Not only are poltergeists noisy, they can also be destructive. Poltergeists have been blamed for shattering glass and setting fires. They have also been known to produce water puddles or slime-filled rooms. Psychic investigator Guy Lyon Playfair has this to say about poltergeists: "They throw rocks around, overturn furniture, set clothing on fire, soak rooms with water, rearrange people's personal belongings and often steal them, transport anything from babies to two-ton

Psychic investigator Guy Lyon Playfair inspects damage to a roof in Sao Paulo, Brazil, apparently caused by poltergeist activity.

Coincidence or Curse?

Eerie events surrounding the *Poltergeist* movies have led many to believe the films were cursed. Four of the movies' stars and one director all died prematurely. Unconfirmed reports that real human skeletons were used in the first film led some people to believe that angry spirits of the deceased caused the curse.

trucks, and generally drive a lot of peace-loving citizens out of their mind."[2]

While poltergeist antics can be troubling, most accounts do not include serious physical injury. Some cases of violence have been reported, however. In a few cases victims have reportedly been dragged or thrown from their beds. Poltergeist victims have also claimed to have been scratched, slapped, or pinched. Some accounts even mention victims having been bitten. These attacks reportedly left animallike bite marks all over the victims' bodies. In one particularly frightening case, **paranormal** investigator Henry Durbin filed this report about two young sisters in Bristol, England:

> Molly said she was bit in the arm, and presently Dobby cried out the same. We saw their arms

bitten about twenty times that evening. Their arms were put out of bed, and they lay on their backs. They could not do it themselves, as we were looking at them the whole time. We examined the bites and found on them the impression of eighteen or twenty teeth, with saliva or spittle all over them in the shape of a mouth. [3]

Poltergeists have also been blamed for the mysterious shaking or moving of furniture and the opening and closing of doors. Marks or writing on floors or walls, appliances turning on and off on their own, and the disruption of electronic items have been connected to poltergeist activity as well. In a few cases poltergeists have even been reported to have caused people to mysteriously rise into the air. While many of these activities may seem ghost-like, **parapsychologists** do not believe poltergeists are the same as ghosts.

Ghosts Versus Poltergeists

Author Pat Fitzhugh writes, "Poltergeist activity is known as a 'disturbance,' whereas ghost-like activity (fog, mist, transparent figures) is known as a 'haunting.' . . . Poltergeists are heard but not seen, whereas ghosts are seen but seldom heard." [4]

One of the main differences between ghosts and poltergeists is that ghosts are usually connected to a certain place, while poltergeists are linked to a specific person. In almost every case of poltergeist activity, the events seem to surround one living per-

Poltergeist activity is reported to include the mysterious moving of furniture and the opening and closing of doors.

son. This person is known as the **agent**. An agent is often a young person between the ages of ten and twenty. Agents are usually under some type of stress. Girls are often, but not always, the targets of poltergeists. An agent who is surrounded by poltergeist activity is usually unaware that he or she is the poltergeist's focus.

Ghosts and poltergeists are not the same thing. For example, ghosts are usually connected to a certain place, while poltergeists are linked to a specific person.

If the poltergeist agent moves to a different place, poltergeist activity often follows the agent to the new area. But a ghost who is known to haunt a specific house usually stays in the same location. This is because the haunted area is most often a place the ghost knew while it was alive.

Poltergeist activity usually builds up over time and then may stop completely—and possibly start up again. In most cases poltergeist **phenomena** usually do not last long. Typical poltergeist activity occurs for only a few days or months at a time, although there have been cases that have lasted much longer. On the other hand, ghost hauntings often go on for years.

Poltergeist Theories

Many theories have been used to explain poltergeist activity. In medieval times poltergeists were thought to be devils or demons that lived inside of people. Later, some people believed that poltergeists were spirits of the dead. They believed these spirits were trying to contact the living from beyond the grave.

Most parapsychologists today believe the stress or anger that an agent feels is what causes poltergeist activity. They think the mental energy that comes from an agent's situation is enough to move objects, make

The Skeptics Speak

In one case that was originally blamed on a poltergeist, investigators discovered that vibrations from a washing machine in an adjoining apartment were the cause of a crystal figurine's movement across a dresser.

noises, start fires, and even create smelly odors. This type of energy is called **psychokinesis** or **PK**. The word *psycho* means "of the mind," while the word *kinesis* refers to the energy that causes movement. Parapsychologists think that internal PK energy may be

A parapsychologist traces chalk around an object to see if it moves during a poltergeist event.

directed toward objects outside the body, thereby causing the disturbances.

Since agents usually do not know they are the cause of the bizarre activity and have no control over it, parapsychologists call their type of PK **recurrent spontaneous psychokinesis** or **RSPK**. Paranormal investigators believe that agents experiencing RSPK project an emotional energy that can cause the movement of an object without their realizing it. In many cases, once the agent's emotional stress or frustration is removed, the poltergeist activity ends. Other investigators believe that PK energy may somehow be connected to electromagnetic forces within Earth. They think human brain waves and electrical impulses from the agent's heart may mesh with those naturally occurring electromagnetic waves and cause PK energy to be released.

Other theories of poltergeist activity that have nothing to do with PK have been studied as well. Skeptics point to natural causes for some disturbances that are blamed on poltergeists. They believe barely detectable earth movements, gas pockets, underground streams, and even human trickery are behind reported poltergeist disturbances. Still others believe that these unusual stories are just that—stories made up by people with overactive imaginations who are looking for attention. Who knows what really brings on these frightening activities? Everyone must make up his or her own mind as to what to believe about these strange and mysterious happenings.

Chapter 2

Flying Objects, Stones, and Fire

O bjects reportedly fly through the air. Stones fall from clear skies. Mysterious fires erupt. These are just a few types of activities reported in poltergeist cases. In many cases exhaustive research has been conducted to discover the cause of the events. Often investigators are unable to pinpoint a specific cause, but the families who have been involved in these incidents feel confident their homes have been invaded by poltergeists.

Noted parapsychologist William G. Roll investigated a case of flying objects at a home in Newark, New Jersey, in 1961. Maybelle Clark had been plagued by objects zooming around her apartment under their own power. Upon Roll's arrival at Clark's apartment,

Clark told Roll she was extremely worried that someone might be hit and injured by one of the flying objects, but Roll tried to squelch her worries. He said, "'It doesn't hit people.' At that instant, a small bottle which had stood on an end table by a sofa hit me squarely in the head."[5]

Flying Objects

The Enfield poltergeist made headlines in London in 1977 due to its flying-object phenomena. Much of the activity surrounded twelve-year-old Janet Harper. Flying toys whizzed throughout the Harper household. Small plastic building bricks and marbles soared in every direc-

Flying objects is one of the most common types of activities reported in poltergeist cases.

tion. A reporter and photographer who visited the Harpers' home to gather information for a newspaper story were surprised when they became a part of the action. For most of the time during their visit nothing mysterious occurred, but as the men got ready to leave they were pelted by flying marbles and plastic bricks. One of the bricks hit the photographer with such force

Investigator Maurice Gross displays some of the smaller items from the Enfield poltergeist case.

that it caused a bruise on his forehead that lasted more than a week. Although Janet was present during this time, the men say they did not see her throw the toys.

Later, in the Enfield case, something else was said to have flown into the air. But this time it was not an object—it was twelve-year-old Janet herself. Reports say Janet was lifted from her bed by an unseen force that caused her to float in the air. In a few instances it was reported that Janet was even trapped against the ceiling for short periods. This floating process which defies gravity is called **levitation**. Two witnesses, who were outside the house at the time, stated they could see Janet through her window. According to the witnesses, Janet hovered in the air surrounded by a flurry of flying books and toys. Was a poltergeist responsible for the activity in Janet's household? Or was it trickery? No one seems to know for sure.

Mysterious Stones

Household items are not the only items that get tossed around during poltergeist disturbances. Many stories of unusual stone throwing have been reported over thousands of years. In 1682 an unseen entity called the stone-throwing devil tormented New Hampshire by pelting residents with stones of all sizes for several days. During that time most people believed that the stone throwing was caused by some sort of peculiar nonhuman source. Since this incident took place over 300 years ago, it is impossible to know for sure if it was caused by poltergeist activity.

A photo taken of Janet Harper on her bedroom floor, allegedly tipped there by poltergeists.

Eleven-year-old Maria José Ferreira of Brazil found herself in the middle of an eerie stone-throwing incident in 1965. A neighbor who had studied psychic phenomena, Jobo Volpe, took Maria into his home after strange happenings had occurred in her presence. Volpe believed Maria was a spiritual **medium**. A medium is a person who is thought to have the ability to communicate with spirits. Immediately upon Maria's arrival at Volpe's home, stones began to fall. The interesting part is that the stones, which seemed to appear from nowhere, were not falling on the outside of the home—they were falling on the *inside*. More than 300 stones fell during Maria's stay. Most of the stones were small and did little damage, but one of them weighed over 8 pounds (3.6kg). That is as much as a junior-size bowling ball. On one occasion Volpe said he watched as a large stone fell from the ceiling. Before it hit the floor, the stone reportedly separated into two pieces. When the pieces were picked up, they immediately snapped back together as if they were magnetized.

Fortunately for those in the home, the stones rarely struck anyone. In one incident, however, reports say a small stone appeared in the air and gently tapped three different people on the top of their heads before falling to the floor. No explanation could be found for these events. Investigators today wonder if Maria might have been a poltergeist agent who unknowingly caused those incidents by a release of RSPK energy.

Perhaps the most amazing stone-throwing story took place in Sumatra in 1928. Paranormal investigator Ivan T. Sanderson sat with friends one evening on the porch of one of their homes. All of a sudden, shiny black rocks began raining down upon the group. Sanderson and his friends searched everywhere but could not discover the source. Confused by this unusual event, Sanderson and his friends tried to figure out what they might do to solve the mystery.

After a while Sanderson came up with an idea. He gathered several of the stones and made marks on them with a piece of chalk. After counting the marked stones, Sanderson and his friends tossed the stones back out into the darkness. The group did not know what to expect, but they were stunned by what happened next. Within minutes another shower of stones peppered the porch. When Sanderson and his friends picked up the rocks, they were shocked to see that every single one of the marked stones had been returned to them. The group was baffled. How could that have happened? The area in which they had thrown the stones was overgrown with weeds and thick brush. It would have been impossible for a human to locate the marked stones that quickly in such an overgrown area. Sanderson and his friends came to the conclusion that poltergeist activity was the only possible explanation.

Fire Starters

Not only do stones suddenly appear in certain poltergeist cases, something much more deadly can also occur without warning—fires. In one 1958 case, a family from Alabama moved more than five times in one month in order to escape the numerous fires that erupted in their homes. Items such as mattresses, televisions, newspapers, and even a loaf of bread mysteriously burst into flames. At one point, one of the children in the family was suspected of starting the fires, but many people reportedly witnessed items bursting into flames all by themselves. Police officer Ben Cooley had this to say about a quilt he saw spontaneously ignite: "I saw it, but I wouldn't have believed it myself if I hadn't seen it." [6]

One of the most startling fire cases attributed to a poltergeist occurred in Macomb, Illinois, in 1948. The events surrounded teenager Wanet McNeil, who was unhappy over her parents' divorce. Paranormal investigators believe that Wanet's anger and uncontrolled emotions produced an RSPK energy that caused numerous fires to ignite in her home. Investigators are convinced that Wanet had no idea she was causing the disturbance and that they came about simply from the kinetic energy in her body.

Many poltergeist disturbances involve unusual stone throwing, whereby people are struck by flying stones coming from no known source.

Small brown spots appeared from nowhere on the walls of Wanet's home before spontaneously bursting into flames. Day after day the mysterious fires appeared. In one week over 200 fires broke out at the home. The family was so afraid the house would burn to the ground if something was not done, they placed buckets of water in every room to put out the flames as they erupted.

Local firefighters were called in to investigate. They determined that no flammable substance was found on the walls. Macomb fire chief Fred Wilson had this to say about the fires: "This whole thing is so screwy and fantastic that I'm ashamed to talk about it. Yet we have at least a dozen reputable witnesses that say they saw brown spots smolder suddenly on the walls and ceilings of the home and then burst into flames."[7]

Eventually, the entire house was consumed by fire, along with two barns and a chicken house. Investiga-

Mysterious Stones Explanation

In 2003 an African village was pelted with over 400 stones. Villagers immediately blamed *thokolosi,* a poltergeist. Investigators discovered the actual cause of the stone showers—meteorite fragments.

tors of all types surrounded the farm looking for answers. Numerous theories such as radiation, flammable fly spray, radio waves, and underground gas pockets were explored, but no concrete answers were ever found. Some say Wanet confessed to setting the fires because she was unhappy about her parents' divorce, but that does not explain the number of people who said they saw fires materialize on walls and ceilings of the home when Wanet was not present in the room. As in many poltergeist cases, there are no clear answers to this disturbance.

Chapter 3

Poltergeist Encounters

One night in the early 1930s, at the Borley Rectory in England, something strange happened. The Reverend Lionel Foyster and his wife Marianne were awakened by a loud crash. Windows in the rectory shattered. Furniture moved from place to place. Loud knocking noises rattled throughout the house. These events were just the beginning of many frightening things to come.

Author Troy Taylor shares more details: "[Marianne Foyster] was thrown from her bed at night, slapped by invisible hands, [and] forced to dodge heavy objects. . . . Soon after, there began to appear a series of scrawled messages on the walls. . . . They seemed to be pleading with Mrs. Foyster, using phrases like 'Marianne, please help.'"[8]

Poltergeist encounters have been reported throughout history in most every part of the world. Numerous people have claimed to witness these frightening and often unexplained events.

Poltergeist encounters have been reported throughout history in most every part of the world. Numerous people have claimed to witness these frightening and often unexplained events.

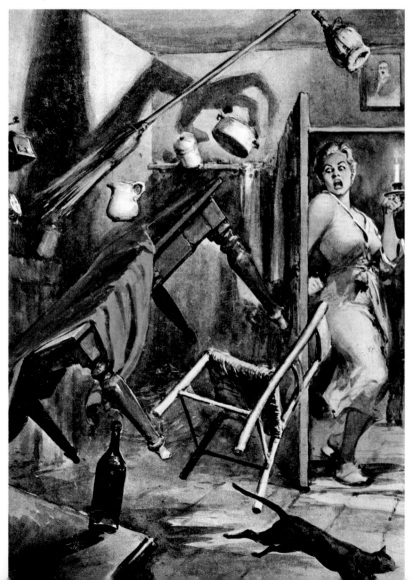

A table rapping session conducted by the Fox sisters, which, they claimed, enabled them to communicate with spirits.

Communicating with a Poltergeist

On a cold winter night in 1848, the Fox family of Hydesville, New York, was just settling into bed when they were awakened by mysterious noises. The sounds of knocks, raps, and moving furniture echoed throughout the house. John Fox and his wife got up and searched the house but could find nothing. Fox's daughters Kate and Maggie also heard the noises. Fox's wife had this to say about the noises:

> On the first night of the disturbance we all got up, lighted a candle and searched the entire house. . . . Although not very loud, [the sounds] produced a jar of the bedsteads and chairs that could be felt when we were in bed. It was a tremulous motion, more than a sudden jar. [The next night] we heard footsteps in the

pantry, and walking downstairs; we could not rest, and I then concluded that the house must be haunted by some unhappy restless spirit.[9]

One night, the Foxes' youngest daughter, Kate, had an idea. She wanted to try to communicate with the **entity**. When she heard several knocks, she clapped her hands and said, "do as I do."[10] Kate clapped four times and the spirit responded with four raps. Soon Kate and her family discovered a way to communicate with the

The Fox sisters: Margaretta, Kate, and Leah.

spirit. They asked questions and the spirit rapped his answers—one rap for "no" and two raps for "yes." By asking a series of questions, the Fox family determined that the spirit was that of a man who had been killed in the house and buried in the cellar years earlier. Several years later some sources reported bits of bone were found beneath the Foxes' cellar, while another report tells of the discovery of an entire human skeleton.

As the Fox sisters grew older, they became famous mediums. People believed the sisters had special powers that enabled them to communicate with spirits. Hundreds of people visited them. They wanted Kate and Margaretta to help them receive messages from their dead friends and relatives.

Years later the sisters were accused of **fraud**. Some people thought they made up the stories about the rappings and their ability to speak to the spirits. Others believed that the incidents at their house in Hydesville were real, but they thought the sisters later faked their abilities in order to stay in the public eye.

The Bottle-Popping Poltergeist

Another unusual poltergeist case revolved around the Herrmann family of Seaford, Long Island. In 1958 Mrs. Herrmann heard a series of popping sounds throughout her house. When she went to investigate, she found all kinds of bottles in almost every room had popped their tops. Not only had their lids come off, the bottles had also fallen over and spilled their contents. Shampoo, perfume, bleach, medicine, paint

Detective Joseph Tozzi sorts through notes and evidence as he works the Herrmann poltergeist case.

thinner, and other liquids made a sticky, smelly mess throughout the Herrmann household.

Several different people witnessed the unusual activities. A member of the Long Island police department, Detective Joseph Tozzi, had this to say about what he saw: "There was a bottle of ink on the south side of the table. A very loud pop was heard and the ink bottle lost its screw top and the bottle left the table in a northeasterly direction. The bottle landed in the living room and the ink spilled on the chair, floor, and on the wallpaper." [11]

Over time more than twenty bottle-popping occurrences took place. Along with the popping bottles, figurines, lamps, and plates were tossed about the

Fox Family Fraud?

Many years after the Hydesville incidents took place, Margaretta Fox admitted that she and her sister had produced the rapping noises to frighten their mother. How did they accomplish this? By cracking their knee and toe joints!

room. Bookcases and tables were also toppled. Many investigators visited the house throughout this period. They wanted to determine what could be causing these disturbances. Building inspectors and electrical engineers searched for answers. A vibration detector was set up in the house to see if some sort of vibrations in the floor might have caused the incidents. Contents of the bottles were examined to make sure nothing had been put in them to cause the eruptions. Technicians even measured radio waves in the area. None of these investigations led to an answer.

Parapsychologist Roll also investigated. Since all other possible causes had been ruled out, Roll suggested that the Herrmanns' twelve-year-old son, Jimmy, might have been playing tricks on the family. Roll noted that the disturbances always took place when Jimmy was at home. Jimmy was watched closely to make sure he was not playing pranks. This theory was ruled out, however, when investigators observed several disturbances, and they could clearly see that Jimmy was not involved. Could twelve-year-old Jimmy have been the poltergeist agent and experienced RSPK? No one knows for sure. The events at the Herrmanns' home lasted about five weeks before disappearing completely.

The Schoolroom Poltergeist

Eleven-year-old Virginia Campbell played a major role in another poltergeist encounter. Virginia had

Jimmy Herrmann, the son in the Long Island, New York, household where poltergeist activity took place in 1958.

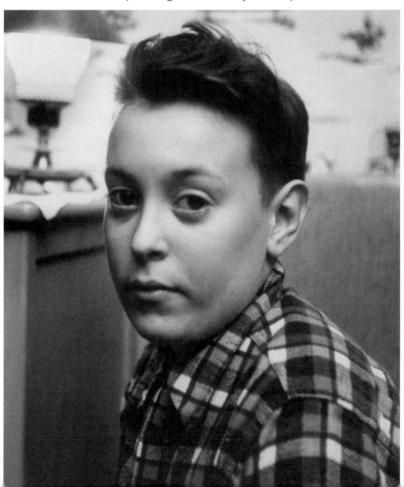

just moved to Scotland with her mother in 1960, and she was not particularly happy in her new home. She missed her father, who had stayed behind in Ireland to sell their home there. A few days after Virginia arrived at her new home, strange things began happening. Large pieces of furniture scooted across the floor, her pillow rotated while her head was resting on it, and knocking noises were heard throughout the house. No one could explain what was happening.

These unusual incidents even followed Virginia to school. Virginia's teacher, Miss Stewart, watched as the lid of Virginia's desk kept opening on its own. Virginia used both hands to try to keep it shut, but she could not stop it from rising. Shortly afterward, Stewart saw the empty desk behind Virginia rise a few inches off of the floor.

A few days later Virginia went up to Stewart's desk for help on an assignment. Roll tells what happened next: "While the teacher was writing and explaining, she suddenly saw the blackboard pointer . . . start to vibrate and move until it reached the edge of the desk. . . . At the same time, Miss Stewart felt a vibrating movement in the desk and [it] began to rotate in a counterclockwise direction." [12]

When Virginia's father arrived from Ireland, Stewart commented that Virginia seemed much more relaxed and happy. All the unusual events ceased. As with many typical poltergeist cases, once the agent's tension goes away, so do the strange happenings.

Chapter 4

Poltergeist Attacks

While most poltergeist cases are simply bothersome, messy, and frightening, in some cases poltergeists have been blamed for serious human injury. In one particular case in 1761, two sisters, Molly and Dobby Giles, were reportedly dragged from their beds on numerous occasions by invisible forces. In one report, investigators claimed that they held tightly to the children's upper bodies while an unexplained power pulled the children by their legs with a mighty force. The children cried out in pain as the men struggled to hold them from the invisible pulling energy. The men's strength was no match for the force, however, and the girls were thrown violently from their beds. Unfortunately for the victims, this is only one of

Reports of poltergeist cases range from those that are simply bothersome and frightening to those that have been blamed for serious human injury.

many cases where poltergeists have been blamed for causing physical harm.

Poltergeist Girl

One of the most frightening and violent poltergeist cases ever recorded was that of a young Romanian girl named Eleonore Zugun. In 1925 eleven-year-old Eleonore was walking to her grandmother's house. On her way Eleonore was delighted to find some money on the ground. Eleonore used the money to buy candy, which she ate on her journey. When Eleonore's grandmother learned that Eleonore had eaten candy bought with the found money, she was horrified. She told Eleonore that the money had probably been left there by an evil spirit. According to her grandmother, since Eleonore had eaten the candy she had purchased with the spirit's money, she now had the *dracu*, or the devil, inside of her. The very next day poltergeist activity surrounded Eleonore.

For the next three years Eleonore was viciously tormented. Author Brian Haughton writes:

> Objects were violently hurled at Eleonore, she was slapped, forced to the ground, tossed out of bed, had her hair yanked out and her shoes filled with water. As if this wasn't enough, from late March 1926, things got even worse. The girl's hands and fingers were constantly pricked as if by needles, and sometimes real needles were found embedded in her flesh. [13]

Bite and scratch marks on the arm of a poltergeist victim, similar in nature to those found on Eleonore Zugun.

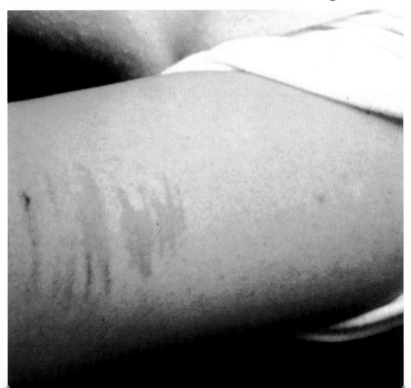

Psychic investigator Harry Price heard about the case and invited Eleonore to visit him in London. Eleonore spent three weeks at Price's laboratory—the National Laboratory of Psychical Research. During that time Price and other scientists reported that they observed bite and scratch marks mysteriously appear on Eleonore's arms and chest. Price obtained a series of photographs and even a film of Eleonore's injuries. After carefully studying the case, Price and the other investigators came to the following conclusion:

> There is not the slightest doubt that our careful experiments, made under ideal scientific conditions have proved that:
>
> a. Markings appeared spontaneously in various parts of Eleonore's body;
>
> b. That Eleonore was not consciously responsible for the production of the marks.[14]

No one knows why Eleonore was subjected to three years of pain and torture, but around the time of Eleonore's fourteenth birthday, all the terrifying phenomena ended. Eleonore went on to live a normal life.

The Amherst Poltergeist

Shocking and violent poltergeist activity was also reported in Canada in 1878. Nineteen-year-old Esther Cox of Amherst, Nova Scotia, was the victim. One night as she and her sister Jennie got ready to go to sleep, they heard a rustling noise. The girls pulled a

The Nova Scotia, Canada, home of poltergeist victim Esther Cox.

box loaded with fabric scraps from under the bed, expecting to find a mouse. But they found a spine-chilling sight instead. As they looked on, the box of scraps rose into the air and bounced around the room.

The next night something even more horrifying happened. Esther and Jennie were in bed when Esther jumped up screaming. Jennie turned on the light and was shocked by the sight of her sister. Parapsychologist Nandor Fodor tells us what Jennie saw: "[Esther's] body began to swell and puffed out to an abnormal size. Soon after, a terrific noise, 'like a peal of thunder' woke everyone in the house. The bedclothes flew off of Esther's bed. . . . An invisible hand cut words into the plaster of the wall, while everyone heard the noise of writing. [The words read:] 'Esther Cox, you are mine to kill.'" [15]

Days later, more mysterious disturbances occurred. Esther reported that she could now hear the spirit's voice and its words frightened her. The voice told Esther that it would burn her house to the ground. Reports say lighted matches began falling from the ceiling and one of Esther's dresses fell from its hook and caught fire. Fortunately for Esther and her family, the fires were extinguished before they could do much damage.

During this time Esther continued to be tortured. The entity was said to have stuck pins all over Esther's body. A visitor to the house, Walter Hubbell, said this about the pins: "They came out of the air from all quarters and were stuck into all the exposed portions of her person, even her head and inside her ears." [16]

The Skeptics Speak

Many experts do not believe the swelling of Esther Cox's body can be blamed on poltergeist activity. It would not be uncommon for the swelling to have been triggered by an infection or allergic reaction.

Along with torturing Esther with pins, the spirit was said to have tried to cut Esther's throat on two occasions. The spirit also supposedly stabbed Esther in the neck with a pair of scissors and in the back with a pocket knife. Items such as forks and potatoes flew across the room and often landed in Esther's direction. Loud slaps were heard followed by the appearance of bright red finger marks on Esther's face.

The horrendous events that took place in the Coxes' home lasted for nearly a year. Esther tried to escape the torment by moving several times, but the disturbances followed her wherever she went. Finally, Esther went to work at a nearby farm. When the farm's barn burned to the ground, Esther was charged with **arson** and sent to jail for a month. It was never clear if Esther intentionally set the fire or if the poltergeist activity that surrounded her was to blame. After Esther's release from jail the poltergeist activity mysteriously ended.

Years later a researcher contacted Esther and wanted to discuss the events, but Esther refused. She said she was afraid that if she talked about the disturbances, they might return.

While the majority of people are skeptical when it comes to the presence of poltergeists, many others claim to have witnessed these disturbances and attacks firsthand. These witnesses are fully convinced poltergeists are real. Investigators often do not have all the answers they would like, so in the majority of cases they simply have to study the evidence presented and speculate on the cause of the disturbance. Along with paranormal explanations, some researchers also continue to focus on naturally occurring causes—such as electromagnetic forces, almost undetectable earth movements, and accumulation of gases beneath the earth—that could possibly explain poltergeist activity. In the end, the presence of poltergeists, along with their antics and injuries, remains a mystery.

Notes

Chapter 1: Noisy Spirits

1. Quoted in Elliot O'Donnell, "Occult Hooligans," HorrorMasters, 2005. www.horrormasters.com/Text/a2249.pdf., p. 1.
2. Quoted in G.H. Playfair, *The Unknown Power.* New York: Simon & Schuster, 1975, p. 4.
3. Quoted in D. Scott Rogo, *The Poltergeist Experience: Investigations into Ghostly Phenomena.* New York: Penguin, 1979, p. 183.
4. Quoted in Pat Fitzhugh, "Poltergeists: The Difference Between Ghosts and Poltergeists," Global Oneness Commitment. www.experiencefestival.com/a/Poltergeists/id/21865, p. 1.

Chapter 2: Flying Objects, Stones, and Fire

5. Quoted in William Roll, *The Poltergeist.* Metuchen, NJ: Scarecrow, 1976, p. 39.
6. Quoted in Troy Taylor, "The Alabama Fire Poltergeist," Ghosts of the Prairie, 2002. www.prairieghosts.com/al_fire.html, p. 2.
7. Quoted in Troy Taylor, "The Macomb Poltergeist," Ghosts of the Prairie, 2002. www.prairieghosts.com/macomb.html, p. 2.

Chapter 3: Poltergeist Encounters

8. Quoted in Troy Taylor, "Borley Rectory: The History of 'The Most Haunted House in England,'" *Ghosts of the Prairie*, 2000. www.prairie ghosts.com/brectory.html, p. 2.

9. Quoted in E.E. Lewis, *A Report of the Mysterious Noises Heard in the House of John D. Fox in Hydesville, Arcadia, Wayne County.* New York: E.E. Lewis, 1848, p. 1.

10. Quoted in Lewis, *A Report of the Mysterious Noises,* p. 2.

11. Quoted in Roll, *The Poltergeist,* p. 16.

12. Quoted in Roll, *The Poltergeist,* p. 87.

Chapter 4: Poltergeist Attacks

13. Quoted in Brian A. Haughton, "Eleonore Zugun—Poltergeist Girl," Mysterious People, 2003. www.mysteriouspeople.com/Eleonore_Zugun. htm, p. 3.

14. Quoted in Nandor Fodor, *The Encyclopedia of Psychic Science.* New Hyde Park, NY: University Books, 1966, p. 416.

15. Quoted in Fodor, *The Encyclopedia of Psychic Science,* p. 292.

16. Quoted in Nandor Fodor, *These Mysterious People.* London: Rider, 1934, p. 4.

Glossary

agent: The person that poltergeist activity surrounds.

arson: A fire set intentionally to cause destruction.

dracu: A Romanian word for "devil."

entity: Something that exists; a living or nonliving being.

fraud: Deliberately deceiving people.

levitation: Defying gravity by floating through the air.

medium: A person who is said to be able to contact and communicate with the dead.

paranormal: Impossible to explain scientifically.

parapsychologists: Scientists who study paranormal activity.

phenomena: Occurrences that are out of the ordinary.

psychokinesis (PK): The movement of items by means of mental energy.

poltergeist: A noisy, often destructive spirit that haunts people by throwing objects, overturning furniture, setting fires, and other types of disturbances.

recurrent spontaneous psychokinesis (RSPK): The movement of items caused by uncontrolled mental energy.

thokolosi: An African word for a type of poltergeist.

For Further Exploration

Books

Anna Claybourne, *Poltergeists? The Evidence and the Arguments.* London: Usborne, 1998. This book covers several poltergeist cases and includes assessments of the facts behind each story.

Stuart A. Kallen, *Poltergeists.* Farmington Hills, MI: Thomson Gale, 2005. This detailed book looks at all aspects of poltergeist phenomena. It includes some cases of historical poltergeists as well as an entire chapter devoted to poltergeist hunters and their investigative practices.

Peter Roop and Connie Roop, *Poltergeists: Great Mysteries, Opposing Viewpoints.* San Diego: Greenhaven, 1988. This is an interesting look at poltergeist phenomena. It includes information about various poltergeist theories advanced by researchers and how their evidence is refuted by skeptics.

Graham Watkins, *Unsolved Mysteries: Ghosts and Poltergeists.* New York: Rosen, 2002. While this book only devotes one chapter to poltergeist phenomena, it discusses scientific theories behind ghosts and poltergeists.

Web Sites

The Atlantic Paranormal Society—TAPS (www.the-atlantic-paranormal-society.com). Investigators for the Sci-Fi Channel's *Ghost Hunter* series fill this Web site with stories, articles, and evidence of paranormal happenings.

The Enigma of American Poltergeists (www.prairie ghosts.com/amer_polt.html). This site consists of links to both famous and little-known poltergeist stories throughout the United States.

The Ghost Club (www.ghostclub.org.uk). Numerous recently investigated cases of poltergeist activity appear on this Web site.

Index

About the Author

Katy S. Duffield has been writing for children and young adults for more than ten years. Her first book, *Farmer McPeepers and His Missing Milk Cows,* published in 2003, was named the Arkansas Diamond Honor Book for 2005–2006. Duffield's work has also appeared in many magazines including *Highlights for Children, Family Fun, Guideposts for Kids, Focus on the Family Clubhouse,* and many others. For more information on her work, visit her Web site at www.katyduffield.com.

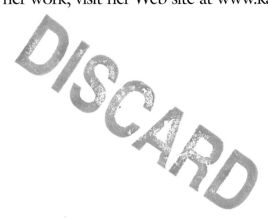